MW00990284

"Best little book about positive attitude I have read. The *Key* has opened doors for me already, and I have only had my copy *one* week. Thank you very much for sharing!"

— Betty Arnold, distributor, Shaklee Products

"I found [*The Ultimate Secret*] at just the right time in my life, and its words of wisdom have been of great comfort to me."

— J. Vitale

"Thank you for writing such a neat book. I am glad to say that the distribution of [*The Ultimate Secret*], one to each new agent, is generating 'Big Bucks.'"

— William W. Klein, American Marketing

"Thank you for *The Ultimate Secret*. It has helped me more than anything else I have *ever* read."

— D. Faast

"I think [*The Ultimate Secret*] is absolutely wonderful! It is really 'the secret' and the absolute truth."

— Betty Dodds, publicist, Literary Promotions Network

The
ULTIMATE SECRET
to GETTING ABSOLUTELY
EVERYTHING YOU WANT

Mike Hernacki

PELICAN PUBLISHING COMPANY
GRETNA 2012

TO WANDA

First published by Berkley Books, 1982, 1988, 2001
Published by arrangement with the author by
Pelican Publishing Company, Inc., 2007

First edition, 1982
Second edition, 1988
Third edition, 2001
First Pelican edition, 2007
English edition in Nigeria, 2007
English edition in India, 2011
Second printing, 2012

Library of Congress Cataloging-in-Publication Data

Hernacki, Mike.
The ultimate secret to getting absolutely everything
you want / Mike Hernacki.
p. cm.
Originally published: Rev. Berkley ed. New York :
Berkley Books, 1988.
ISBN-13: 978-1-58980 486-9
1. Success.I. Title.

BJ1611.H4472001
158—dc212001035184

Book design by Tiffany Kukec
Cover design by Pyrographx

Printed in the United States of America
Published by Pelican Publishing Company, Inc.
1000 Burmaster Street, Gretna, Louisiana 70053

CONTENTS

Introduction   vii

1. The Secret Link   1

2. A Simple Principle   13

3. What the Principle Says—and
   What It Doesn't Say   31

4. The Key: Willingness   39

5. Where It Starts: With You   45

6. What You Need   59

7. What You Don't Need   65

8. How the Principle Works   79

9. What Keeps the Principle
   from Working   99

10. The Tyranny of the
    Accomplished Goal   113

11. The Endless Joy of the Journey   119

12. Begin It Now   125

INTRODUCTION

If you're finding the title of this book a little hard to swallow, I don't blame you. After all, how can one slim volume hold a Secret so huge it can bring you everything—absolutely everything—you want? How can a writer make such a claim? The answer is simple: I have lived this Secret for some twenty years now, and have proven that it works.

I wrote the first version of *The Ultimate Secret* in 1982. At the time, I had just started to achieve some success after many years of frustration. When I analyzed what was working for me, I discovered I was unconsciously using the principle explained in this book. This principle is so powerful, so effective, the only words I could find to describe it were, "The Ultimate Secret to Getting Absolutely Everything You Want."

"IF YOU'RE SO DAMN SMART, WHY AIN'T YOU RICH?"

My father had a hard life. He was forced to quit elementary school and go to work to help support his large immigrant family. He got his "education" in the streets, sweatshops, and factories of pre-Depression Detroit. Everything he ever had, he *earned*—with a combination of hard work and lessons he learned in the real world. Dad had little patience with self-proclaimed experts who gave advice based on what they had studied rather than their experience. When such an "expert" tried to tell him what to do, he liked to say, "If you're so damn smart, why ain't you rich?"

My father died before this book was written. If he'd

been alive when he saw the title, he'd have been skeptical—and with good reason. In 1982, I was only mildly successful, had a very short list of achievements, and while the IQ tests said I was smart, I was far from rich. The Ultimate Secret was something I had just discovered, and not yet had a chance to put to work consciously for an extended period. Today, nearly twenty years later, I've had ample opportunity to use the Secret and if I were now able to give my father a report on my real-world results, I'd say, "Dad, the title is true. I've used this Secret to create a life that has absolutely everything I want."

Do I have everything I could *possibly* want? No. Everything I'll *ever* want? No. But without boasting or exaggerating I can say this: I live exactly where I want. I'm financially independent, having retired in my early 50s. I'm happily married to the perfect woman for me. I'm healthy and physically fit. I spend my days doing what I like to do. And none of this has happened by accident or coincidence. I've created it all by consciously using The Ultimate Secret.

As you read this book, you'll see there's nothing extraordinary about me. Plenty of people have far more brains, talent, and ambition. I may be above average, but not all that much. In fact, my ordinariness is even more evidence of the tremendous power of this Secret. If I could use it to create the life I want, so can you.

THE MORE THINGS CHANGE . . .

A lot has changed in the nearly twenty years since this book was first written. When my editor called to tell me a new edition was being planned for 2001, she said, "You've quoted some numbers, especially in the first chapter, that are ancient history now. Make sure you update them." So I did new research and was treated to some interesting surprises.

In 1982, I found 196 books on how to become

wealthy. Today there are **976** offered by one online bookseller alone. Two decades ago, I found 497 titles on the subject of success. Today I find **over 4,000**. So we see that if you're the kind of person who reads self-help books, as I was, you've got many times more of them at your disposal than ever before. If you add in the explosion of self-help titles in audiotapes, video-tapes, and software, not to mention the thousands of websites that didn't even exist back then, you are soon overwhelmed by the plethora of resources available to help you succeed.

But are all these success aids helping more people succeed? Well, yes—and no. Let me explain.

Success is hard to measure, so I chose to use a person's net worth as a yardstick, simply because money, while not the only component of success, is the easiest to count. Twenty years ago, a net worth of one million dollars was generally accepted as the mark of a financially successful person. Today I'm not so sure.

Adjusted for inflation, you'd need well over two million dollars to be just as rich as a 1980s millionaire. Some financial experts claim that you really can't call yourself rich today unless you have at least three million bucks. Even so, a million dollars is still a powerful symbol of affluence. Currently, the most popular American television show is *Who Wants to Be a Millionaire?* while *The Millionaire Next Door* has lived on the bestseller lists for years.

In my original research, I found that according to the 1980 census, there were some 400,000 millionaires in the United States. Since the 2000 census is not yet tabulated, I had a hard time finding a comparable number. But the 1990 census pegged the ranks of millionaires near 1.5 million and by the late 1990s, demographers were estimating that the number of U.S. *households* (as opposed to individuals) with one million dollars' net worth had soared to five million. Of course, so many people now have substantially all their assets committed to highly volatile stocks that this number changes literally every day.

To keep our comparisons accurate, we should eliminate all those whose net worth is below two million, since that's what 1980s millionaires need today to live as well as they did then. By most estimates, this cuts the ranks in half, more or less. For simplicity's sake, we can conclude there are about five times as many millionaires today as there were twenty years ago: 400,000 then; 2,000,000 now. In that time span, the overall population has grown by about 20 percent, so the actual multiple is somewhat lower than five times the previous number.

What do all these numbers tell us? First, there are many more financially successful people today than there were when this book was first written—both in raw numbers and in percentage of the population. Second, the number of people who can call themselves "rich" by 1980's standards is still quite small:

less than 1 percent of the population. Third, while the ranks of the wealthy have grown, they have not grown as fast as the number of books, tapes, software programs, and websites that are designed to help people become wealthy. Things have changed, but in a larger sense, they have remained the same: There's still a huge gap between learning how to become successful and actually doing it. Today, as it did twenty years ago, The Ultimate Secret fills that gap.

For this reason, I decided to leave the original text intact. Some of the numbers are different, as you have seen, and some of the examples may sound a bit out of date. But the underlying message and the Secret itself are the same. The only major difference is that in 1982 I felt, I believed, I sensed *intuitively* that the Secret works. Today I know *from experience* that it does.

Now it's your turn to find out for yourself.

CHAPTER ONE

The Secret Link

What do you want? A better job? A happy marriage? An education? A new home? Good health? Fame? Fortune? Success?

Whatever you want, you can have. Whether it's large or small; whether it's near at hand or seems impossibly far away, you can have it.

To get what you want, all you need is to know the simple, but powerful, secret explained in this book. To get absolutely everything you want, you don't have to study anything, meet anyone, go anywhere or do anything in particular. I repeat: To get what you want, you don't have to *do* anything. Simply knowing the secret is enough.

How can I make these claims? On the basis of my own experience. For over twenty years, I was an avid reader of so-called "how-to" books, especially the kind that describe how to become rich and successful. I devoured every word and did everything those books suggested. I followed the formulas. I trained myself to think positively. I set goals. I fed my subconscious mind with suggestions for wealth and success. Yet I found that after twenty years of reading millions of words, after twenty years of trying what those well-meaning books instructed, I was not measurably closer to being either rich or successful than I was when I picked up my first how-to book. The reality of this failure haunted me. Why after all those years was I still broke, still struggling, still unsuccessful?

Was I thick-headed? Looking back at my school

years, I recalled that I'd always done well; I'd gotten A's and B's. I'd earned a bachelor of arts degree in English and a law degree. And on intelligence tests, I'd always scored well above the average. So, I wasn't thick-headed.

Did I lack ambition? Well, I had ambition enough to start my own advertising business, despite having no capital and only one client. I had ambition enough to drag myself through four years of law school at night, while running my business during the day. Yes, I had plenty of ambition.

Was I lazy? Being honest with myself, I could admit that work hadn't been my favorite activity. But I certainly did enough of it. I put in a lot of hours at my desk, often working nights and weekends. I took good care of my family, my home, my clothes, all my possessions. I wasn't lazy.

Maybe I was just plain unlucky. But reviewing my

life thoroughly, I saw that I'd never suffered a great misfortune. I'd never gone bankrupt, had a major accident, or even broken a bone. I wasn't unlucky.

So, I was reasonably intelligent and ambitious, worked hard, and had my full share of good luck; but the wealth and success promised in those how-to books continued to elude me. I was determined to find out why. I then began a search that took me down some interesting paths.

In this search, I soon learned that I was not alone in my feelings of failure. At the library, I found listings for 196 different books having to do with becoming wealthy and 497 separate titles on the subject of success. There were hundreds more on salesmanship, motivation, and positive thinking. Mind you, these were the books on hand in just one medium-sized library.

I asked the librarian how many people had read these books. She told me that without contacting each publisher individually it would be impossible to determine how many copies of these books had been sold. And even then the publishers could only guess as to how many people read each copy. After some checking, however, we were able to come up with a conservative estimate: *tens of millions* of copies of how-to books had been sold. With pass-along readership, that number could be multiplied several times.

Later I chanced upon a magazine article about millionaires. The article noted that a personal net worth of one million dollars or more is generally accepted to be a sign of wealth and success in the United States. It also noted that, according to the Census Bureau, in 1980, there were about 400,000 millionaires in the country. Of that number, however, over half were farmers whose main assets—their farms—had appreciated greatly in value in recent years, making their owners millionaires "on paper."

Fewer than 50,000 of the millionaires were under the age of thirty-five. Of these, only a few thousand had "made" the money themselves. The others—including practically all of the farmers—had inherited it.

At the time of the 1980 census, the U.S. had over 226 million people, which means the total number of millionaires made up less than 2 percent of the population. And self-made millionaires amounted to a small fraction of 1 percent.

This was a startling statistic and as I mulled it over, a realization hit me with the force of an electric shock! It occurred to me that, in a marvelous environment where people are free to pursue their fortunes—in a country acknowledged to be the wealthiest on earth, a country whose political and economic systems present the best opportunities for self-made wealth and success in the world—only a tiny percentage had actually reached the traditionally accepted measure of wealth, a million dollars. Of those, only a much tinier group had done it on their own. And of those, a much, much smaller group had done it relatively quickly—before age thirty-five.

I began to wonder about the overwhelming majority who did not become millionaires. Were all of these people uninspired or unmotivated to achieve? Certainly many lacked inspiration and motivation. Yet I had reason to believe that *millions* of them were at least motivated enough to buy and read a book on the subject of becoming successful. Millions of people had read how to become a millionaire, yet only a very few had actually done it. All the rest—the great majority—must be like me: still wanting, still looking, still trying, but not getting the wealth the books promised.

Just like me (perhaps just like you?) the great majority of those who read how-to books would have to be classified as "failures."

This realization gnawed at me. Why did so many of us fail? What secret link, what invisible connection between learning how to do something and the actual accomplishment of it, was missing? And what about the people who had never formally "learned" what to do? What about those who had never read a how-to book, yet achieved great wealth anyway? What secret did those people know that I and the millions of other readers of how-to books didn't know?

After years of searching, I finally found the answer—interestingly enough, within my own self. I found that there *is* a secret link. It's the simple principle that you will learn in this book. The principle is so powerful that, without exaggeration, I have called it "The Ultimate Secret to Getting Absolutely Everything You Want"—and the many thousands of people who have already read and heard me speak about it agree. Without this principle, you can accomplish little. With it, you can accomplish anything you want. Anything.

Everyone, yourself included, uses this principle at one time or another, usually without being aware of it.

Whenever you have accomplished something important, you have used The Ultimate Secret. Whenever you have overcome difficult obstacles, you have used The Ultimate Secret. It's not necessary to be aware of the Secret to use it successfully. But people who *are* aware of it achieve large measures of wealth, success, and happiness.

The best part about The Ultimate Secret is that its possibilities and rewards are limitless: no one has a patent on it; no one has exclusive rights to it; no one can wear it out or use it up. You can begin using it any time. No matter how old you are, no matter how poor or uneducated, no matter what your condition in life, it's not too late for you to begin using it today.

The principle is as old as mankind, yet at this moment, for you, it may be as fresh and new as the day it was discovered. For you, today, it's just as powerful as ever, just as capable of delivering everything you want.

And here it is.

CHAPTER TWO

A Simple Principle

I was once sitting in an empty hallway of the federal courthouse in a large Midwestern city. That day, the courts were not in session. The judges were conducting pretrial conferences and other matters "in chambers," so only a few lawyers were about. I was one of the lawyers, waiting for my pretrial conference to begin.

As I sat there, two attorneys entered the hallway; they were talking about a large lawsuit, which they had obviously just settled. The two men were about the same age, though one of them was considerably taller and more distinguished-looking than the other.

They were physically quite different in appearance but were dressed about the same, wearing neatly tailored three-piece suits.

"I'm glad we got this settled so quickly," the shorter man said. "I'm closing my practice, and this case was the last major item for me to finish."

"Closing your practice?" the other asked. "Why?"

The first man flashed a big grin. "Because I'm moving to Florida."

"How I envy you," the taller attorney said. "I've wanted to move to Florida for years. I'm tired of the noise and the traffic and the cold weather here."

"Then why don't you leave?"

"Oh, I can't move now," he lamented. "My practice is established. My family is rooted here. I have a home, a mortgage and a hundred other strings tying me to this city."

The shorter man was silent a moment, then said, "That's interesting. I, too, have an established practice here. I have a family, a home, all those things you do. But I'm moving anyway."

Suddenly, the taller man's face reddened, and his anger flared. "Then you're just . . . throwing away everything," he said, almost shouting. "And you're a damned fool!" With this, he turned sharply on his heel and strode away, his footsteps making angry echoes down the empty marble hall.

As the shorter attorney shrugged and walked in the other direction, I thought about what had just taken place. These men seemed to be in almost identical situations. They were in the same profession, were close in age, had similar responsibilities and seemed to have the same desire. Both wanted to move to Florida, yet one was excitedly on his way, accomplishing his desire, while the other, in frustration and bitterness, was not. Exactly what was the difference between the two?

I figured that both lawyers surely knew what was

involved in such a move: giving up an established business, uprooting a family, facing the possibility of higher living costs and fewer professional opportunities in the new location—plus who knows what other, unforeseeable difficulties. Both men knew what was involved, yet only one was actually making the move. I wondered why, and filed the question in the back of my mind, hoping I could answer it one day.

Another time, I attended a lecture being given by a man who had made millions of dollars speculating in commodities. Along with several hundred other people, I had paid five dollars to hear how to make a fortune in the commodities markets using the system developed by this highly successful trader.

The air in the packed meeting room was charged with excitement. We all felt as if we were being let in on a valuable secret that would make us all rich. By the middle of the lecture, the speaker had built up a full head of steam, explaining his charts, talking about margins and contracts and the different kinds of orders he placed with his broker.

Suddenly a spectator near the back of the large room stood up and said, "Hey, wait a minute. From what I can see, all this speculation is very risky business. Don't you realize that you can lose every penny you have—and then some?"

The millionaire responded without hesitating. "Why, yes. I certainly do realize that."

"Then why do you continue to speculate?"

"I don't know exactly why," the lecturer answered. "I just know I'm willing to take the risk."

"Well, I'm not," the spectator snapped.

The rich man smiled, paused a moment, and said, "That might be why I'm giving this lecture and you're paying for it." The audience exploded with laughter as the spectator blushed and sat down. He didn't ask another question that evening.

For me, the rest of the lecture was a blur as I focused on the wealthy man's remark: "That might be why I'm giving this lecture and you're paying for it." I couldn't help thinking that this one remark actually held the answer to other "why" questions—questions I had been struggling with for years: Why, despite all my reading and efforts, was I still unsuccessful? Why, despite the sales of millions of how-to books, were so many other people unsuccessful too? Why does one man pull up his roots and pursue his dream with a smile on his face, while another buries *his* dream in bitterness? Why does one man risk all he owns on a pork belly contract, while another shrinks at the thought?

It wasn't until a long time later that the answer—and The Ultimate Secret—came to me, in a most extraordinary and unexpected way.

WHATEVER IT TAKES

Regular surveys consistently show that a large percentage of the people employed in the United States are unsatisfied with their jobs all of the time. For years, I was part of that unfortunate group.

In the years after finishing college, I tried a number of jobs and started a number of careers. My training qualified me to become a schoolteacher, so my first several jobs were in teaching. Though I liked teaching well enough, I saw the classroom as a dead end and the salary as a constant obstacle to my ever becoming affluent. Since I had a certain amount of creative ability, I entered the field of advertising, which promised more in the way of advancement and money. But for me, the promotions and the big money never came, and so I went to law school, thinking that the legal profession *really* offered the kind of success I was looking for.

I found the practice of law to be difficult, depressing, and lacking the kind of excitement depicted in the movies and on television. Hoping to find some excitement in my work, and still have an opportunity to earn a lot of money, I became a stockbroker. Unfortunately, though the excitement and the money were certainly there, the work itself was not for me, and I couldn't get involved with what was going on around me.

After fourteen years of studying and working and looking, I had still not found where I belonged. I felt frustrated, discouraged, stuck.

Then one day I suddenly became very ill. I could barely breathe and had to be rushed to the hospital in the middle of the night. The emergency room doctor took X rays, ran some tests and diagnosed my problem as pneumonia. He referred me to another doctor, who diagnosed the disease as pleurisy and suggested I see a lung specialist. The specialist ran more tests and concluded that I had a virus of some sort. He prescribed drugs and bed rest.

The drugs didn't work very well, but the bed rest gave me an opportunity to think, read, and contemplate what I wanted to do with my life.

My body responded poorly to the treatment, and over several months I progressed only a little. A friend suggested that my problem might be psychosomatic—in other words, that it originated in my mind. At first, I rejected the notion, but as my convalescence dragged on, I began to wonder if my friend had been right. I decided to investigate.

I found a book that gave the possible mental origins of various physical problems. Turning to the section on lung diseases, I read: "Maladies of the lungs and difficulty in breathing are a sign of unfulfilled passions, of unrealized dreams."

Naturally, I asked myself if I did indeed have any unfulfilled passions, or dreams that as yet were unrealized. A few thoughts came to mind, such as my continuing desire to be wealthy and successful. Yet I had never thought of myself as going about with unfulfilled *passions*. The only thing I ever really wanted desperately was . . . aha!

At that moment, my entire problem—and its solution—immediately became clear to me. I was sick in my lungs because all of my adult life, my secret ambition had been to become a professional writer. Yet, for many reasons, I had never allowed myself to pursue that ambition.

If you're looking for reasons *not* to become a writer, there are plenty of them: the work is hard, and for most writers the pay is quite low. Writing is not as prestigious as law, or some of the other professions I had practiced. My excuses were endless, and seemingly sound. And thus my passion had remained unfulfilled, my dream unrealized.

At that moment, I knew that I had to quit my current job and start writing for a living. In a split second, I decided to do it. By the next morning, my lung problem began to clear up. I went back to work for several days, until I got up the courage to let my boss know I was leaving. By the time I said, "I quit," my "virus" was gone, and I was breathing free.

As so often happens, however, the solution to one set of problems is the touchstone for a whole new set. Mine began immediately: money problems, creativity problems, difficulties with learning a craft and making it pay at the same time. But I soon realized that I loved it. For the first time in my life, I enjoyed the process of what I was doing. And I enjoyed the work itself—not just the money or rewards the work brought. I had, at long last, found my right place.

Early in my new writing career, I resolved to make a success of it. Because I loved the work so much, I wanted the privilege of doing it as long as I chose to. That meant I would have to become successful at it. I had no idea *how* to go about becoming a successful writer. I just knew it was what I wanted to do.

So I did it. Obstacles arose, and I overcame them. Problems surfaced, and I solved them. People discouraged me, and I ignored them. Sooner than I had expected, the successes began to come. And soon thereafter, so did the money. Before long, I was more successful at writing than I had been at anything else. I was earning more than I had as an advertising man, attorney, or stockbroker. I was, in fact, earning many times more than the average writer. I had finally accomplished what all those how-to books had said I could do.

Having achieved some prominence in my field, I was asked to put together a guide—a how-to book—on becoming a successful writer. It seemed like a good idea, and a way for me to make a contribution to the lives of others who were struggling to succeed, so I sat down to do it. But when I reviewed my writing career up to that point, I realized that I had no clear idea exactly how I'd gotten to where I was. Every time I checked my records as to how or when something had been done, I found that my memory of it was almost completely inaccurate. Most important, I hadn't knowingly used any of the "success" methods suggested in the how-to books. I just did what I did, and it worked. But how it worked, I could not say.

Then, as I sat at my word processor, grappling with the problem of how to explain the method to my success, a tiny light seemed to flick on in my head. The light grew, and in seconds I experienced a realization so intense that it was exhilarating and painful all at once—exhilarating, because of how instantly clear it made everything; painful because I suddenly knew how much I'd missed by not seeing it sooner.

In that moment, I realized that the *method* of doing something, the how-to of it, doesn't matter. What matters is something totally different, totally unrelated to the process of succeeding. In that moment, I recalled the words of the successful commodities trader who had said, "I just know I'm willing to take the risk."

It occurred to me that for success in commodities speculation the critical element is risk, and indeed to be in it at all, you *must* expose yourself to that element. To succeed, you must be, as that man was, willing to take the risk.

At that moment I also remembered the attorneys in the courthouse hallway. Both wanted to move to Florida. But if you want to move—to Florida or anywhere else—you must give up what you have at home. You must be willing to give up something in order to get something. One of those men was willing, the other wasn't. *That* was the difference between them.

I realized that in trying to write my how-to book, I

had finally stumbled onto a principle, a truth so simple and obvious that most people go through their entire lives without seeing it. Quickly, the words of the principle formed in my mind. And I typed them out, thus:

In order to accomplish something, you must be willing to do whatever it takes to accomplish it.

The Florida-bound lawyer was willing to close his office, move his family, and absorb the costs of starting over. The speculator was willing to put up his entire net worth and risk more than he had. The writer, Mike Hernacki, was willing to quit a good job, give up salary and benefits, and enter a field where a good percentage of its full-time practitioners lived below the poverty line. What these men had in common was their willingness to do whatever was necessary to accomplish their goals.

With their willingness, they were practicing this

principle. Because of their willingness, they were being successful. Ironically, none of them may have been aware of their willingness at the time. I know I certainly wasn't. But as you'll find, that's one of the best parts of The Ultimate Secret: it works whether you're aware of it or not. It's automatic.

Let's look at it again:

In order to accomplish something, you must be willing to do whatever it takes to accomplish it.

CHAPTER THREE

What the Principle Says—
and What It Doesn't Say

The principle says you must be *willing* to do whatever it takes to reach your goal. This is it—the whole Secret—and contrary to what you might have read or heard before, *it stops there!* It demands nothing more of you.

But that's only part of the message. Another extremely important part of the message lies in what the principle does *not* say. The principle does not say that you must actually *do* whatever it takes. It does not say that you have to physically take on every single task necessary for the accomplishment of what you want. It does not demand any specific action. This is the part of The Ultimate Secret most people fail to understand. That's why they buy so many books and take so many classes on what to do and how to do it. They think actual, physical *doing* is the key. It's not.

To comprehend this fully, it will help us to look at some of the differences between the Western and Eastern cultures. In the Western world, chiefly the Americas and Western Europe, we're accustomed to *action*. We're doers, achievers. We believe that to accomplish something, we must physically *do* something. Our educational systems are focused on teaching people how to solve problems. This can be valuable, but only up to a certain point: the point where physical action *cannot* accomplish a goal.

The way we Westerners think, we find it hard to imagine a situation where action cannot accomplish a desired result. Yet there are many such situations in all of our lives.

Let's take a simple one. Let's say you'd just like to be

happy. That's a worthy goal. But what can you *do* to achieve happiness? Well, if you're unhappy about being poor, you could make a lot of money. Would that work? I'm afraid not. Money is nice to have, but it's no guarantee of happiness. If it were, all rich people would be happy, and we know that this simply isn't so.

Suppose you're unhappy being single. Well, you could get married, but as the divorce statistics show, plenty of married people are quite miserable.

If you're unhappy where you live, you could move to a tropical paradise. Well, Hawaii is a tropical paradise and the amount of drug abuse in that state is a matter of deep concern to Hawaiians. And drug abuse is hardly a sign of happiness.

The point is, there's nothing you can *do* to become happy. You can only *be* it. People who *are* happy often realize with delightful surprise that they have somehow achieved happiness without *doing* a thing to get it.

Let's look at an example in which *you* accomplished something without any action whatsoever. When you were a child, there were many things your parents didn't want you to do: play in dangerous places, go about with mischievous friends, stay out after dark. We all can remember such a list. Now, recall a situation in which you *didn't* do one of those things on the list, despite great temptation. For whatever reason, you just decided to obey your parents and stay home when you wanted to go out, or not make yourself available to those friends your parents disapproved of. What happened? Well, if your parents were anything like mine, they were surprised—and pleased. Maybe they complimented you or even gave you a reward.

In that situation, you accomplished a number of items: you caused your parents pleasure, you got a reward or avoided a punishment, and perhaps you simply felt good about yourself. Yet to accomplish these things, you *did* nothing. Your non-action was just as capable of producing real results as action would have been.

The truth is, when it comes to getting results, *intention* is more important than action. What you make up your mind to do is more important than what you actually do. If you choose to begin using The Ultimate Secret, this is where you start, with an *intention.* When you form an intention and keep fast to it, you will eventually achieve the results you want.

When you were a child, the results you achieved in not misbehaving came out of your intention— whether it was fully conscious or not—to be the kind of child your parents wanted, to get a reward, or to avoid a punishment. The results came out of what you *wanted* to be, not out of what you did.

In that instance, the results came from something that was deep inside you. And so it is whenever you use the Secret. Your intention is born in your pride, your desire to excel, your need to improve yourself.

This intention is much, much more important than the actions which flow from it.

In the same way, happiness comes out of your intention to be happy, your *willingness* to be happy, not out of making money, getting married, moving to paradise or *doing* any one of the dozens of things you possibly could to achieve happiness.

There is a lesson in this, a lesson that shows us the key to our Ultimate Secret.

CHAPTER FOUR

The Key: Willingness

Let's review our original principle, which says that to get what you want, you must be *willing* to do whatever it takes to get it. The essence of the principle—the key to it—is the idea of willingness. According to one dictionary's definition, willingness is "a frame of mind that is open to every possible demand, without judgment, reservation or refusal."

As with happiness, you don't have to do anything to achieve willingness. It's a frame of mind. You just have to be willing. There's nothing you have to learn, no one you have to meet, and no process involved in getting it. You get it by having it.

Note that willingness is an *open* frame of mind. This is very important. An open mind is receptive to the possible, the untried, the unproven. It doesn't make judgments. It doesn't make excuses for why things cannot be. It doesn't refuse what is asked of it, no matter how illogical the request may seem.

You may be thinking that, right now, what you want is so far away or so difficult to get that nothing short of a miracle will bring it to you. Never fear. A miracle, also according to a standard dictionary definition, is "an extremely outstanding or unusual event, thing or accomplishment."

You don't need scientific proof to conclude that the thing that enables miracles to take place is the open mind. The miracles of electronics, space travel, and modern medicine did not begin in closed minds. They were born in minds that were "open to every possible demand, without judgment, reservation, or refusal." They were born in willingness.

I might add that, for every open-minded scientist who worked on making these miracles happen, there were many closed-minded scientists who maintained that those "miracles" simply could *not* happen; that miracles as such were beyond the laws of nature. Eventually, the closed-minded ones learned that we are just beginning to discover the laws of nature, that today's fantasy can be tomorrow's fact.

In order to experience "an extremely outstanding or unusual event, thing or accomplishment"—a miracle—in your life, you must have an open mind. You must not judge or refuse. You must be willing—willing to do whatever it takes. And by extension, without doubt, you *will* make miracles happen in your life.

Despite all this talk about miracles, this subject is not in the realm of the mystical or magical. It's real. Remember, the definition doesn't say a miracle is supernatural, only that it is something outstanding or unusual. Real people, with standard human weaknesses and frailties, use this key—willingness—every day, to accomplish real, actual miracles. You can too.

If you're the hard-nosed, skeptical type, and words like "miracle" put you off, I ask that you keep an open mind for just a few minutes—until you finish reading this book. It's not hard to do, and it's a small price to pay for what will ultimately be a great reward. I promise.

CHAPTER FIVE

Where It Starts: With You

To get what you want, you must recognize something that at first may be difficult, even painful to look at. You must recognize that *you alone* are the source of all the conditions and situations in your life. You must recognize that whatever your world looks like right now, *you alone* have caused it to look that way. The state of your health, your finances, your personal relationships, your professional life—all of it is *your* doing, yours and no one else's.

Don't be surprised if you find yourself denying this. While people in general will readily accept responsibility for their successes, few can accept their failures or their self-imposed limitations with the same open arms.

"I can't help it I was born poor," they claim. The response to it is this: That might be, but at birth were you condemned to stay poor throughout your life? How many people were born poor yet went on to achieve great wealth? Some of the largest corporations in the world still bear the names of these people.

"A black person has all the cards stacked against him," people say. The response is this: That might be, but how many black Ph.D.'s are there? How many black mayors and business executives? These successful black people had the cards stacked against them as much as anyone else—in some cases, even more.

"It's not my fault I'm handicapped," others say. That *is* unfortunate. But does handicapped mean helpless? Some years ago, a young man ran from one coast of Canada to the other—on one leg. Every year the President of the United States gives awards to outstanding handicapped Americans. In a recent ceremony, he honored a business executive who had built a successful career while supporting a family, despite being blind *and* in a wheelchair.

Another common excuse is, "I've got too many responsibilities, too many people relying on me." That might be, but how many women, for example, invented new products, founded great institutions, wrote great books, even made great fortunes, all with families relying on them? These women found the time and the energy to make their miracles happen, anyway.

Ralph Waldo Emerson, possibly the greatest philosopher America has ever produced, said, "All successful men have agreed in being causationists." In other words, they see themselves as the *cause*, not the *effect*, of what happens in their lives. Unsuccessful people believe themselves to be the effect.

I now ask you, at this moment, perhaps for the first

time ever, to look carefully at any situation in your life and be honest about it. If you are honest with yourself, you will eventually see that, *either consciously or unconsciously*, you set it up to be that way. Whether you're aware of it or not, you've allowed that situation to remain as it is, even though you've had the ability to change it all along.

As a professional writer, I quite often have the following kind of exchange with people:

"You're a writer? What interesting work that must be."

"Yes, it is."

"I envy you. I've longed to be a writer for years."

"Then why don't you become one?"

"What? And quit my job?"

"Yes, why not?"

"Well, I might hate my job, but it does pay the bills, and the benefits are too good to give up, and with my seniority, I can retire in ten or fifteen years. *I can't quit now.*"

Notice the italicized sentence. This person (and believe me, there are millions like him) actually has convinced himself that the situation is out of his control, that he no longer has the power or ability to change it. He honestly believes that something else, something or someone other than himself is the cause of his predicament, and he is the effect of it. Yet the truth—which he cannot or will not see—is directly the opposite.

For many years, I've known a woman who has gradually become bitter about many lost opportunities. She could have had an exciting career, she claims, if only she didn't have to take care of her widowed mother. She could have married and led a full life, she laments, but her mother has needed her.

Out of curiosity, I once asked her mother about this. The elderly lady shook her head and replied, "Of course, I rely on my daughter and would miss her if she left, but I don't need her that much. In fact, I'd love to see her married and happy. She could take a new job or a husband tomorrow, but *she thinks she can't, so she doesn't do it."*

Again, notice the italicized statement. The limitation is in that unfortunate woman's mind. And she has held on to this belief, even though, according to her mother, she has been told more than once to go and seek the things she pines for.

Another woman I know fled her native country, Czechoslovakia, not long after the morning she woke up to find a Soviet tank parked in front of her house. Once she secured permanent residency in the United States, she rented an apartment in an attractive part of San Diego. She thoroughly enjoyed the apartment and planned to live there indefinitely. Then one day, she received a notice that the apartment complex was scheduled to be converted to condominiums. Her choices were limited: she could buy her apartment or move.

As yet unfamiliar with the English language, she asked a neighbor to explain the situation fully. He shrugged his shoulders and said, "I'm in the same boat. Either we put up a lot of cash for a down payment—which neither you nor I have—or we get out. The apartment owners really aren't giving us any choice."

Later, in telling me the story, the woman said, "When my neighbor told me I had no choice, I got angry. I thought, This is America. I risked everything to move here, just so I could have a choice. There must be a way for me to get what I want."

And so the immigrant sought the advice of others. One of her friends, who was in the real estate business, showed her that, as an existing tenant, she had the right to buy her apartment at an advantageous price and with very liberal financing. Stretching her budget to the limit, she bought her apartment, then later sold it at a huge profit. In the process, she found the field of real estate so fascinating that she decided to learn as much as she could about it.

That was some years ago. Today she is a highly successful commercial real estate broker, drives a luxury car, wears custom-tailored suits, and by every measure, has made the American Dream a reality for herself. I asked her what happened to the neighbor who first advised her that she had no choice.

"I don't know," she replied. "He moved out just before I closed the deal on my place. I felt sorry for him. Here he was, born and raised in America, where people have more choices than anywhere—and he thought that someone else had taken his choice away."

These stories are true, and their message is clear: *You* are the cause, the source of everything that happens in your life. When you recognize this, once and for all, you unleash a powerful force. Once you see that everything that exists for you now is your creation and no one else's, then you'll see that everything that *can* or *will* exist in the future is your creation also.

This recognition of yourself as a powerful source of creation puts you consciously into the driver's seat—a *place you've been all along,* though perhaps unconsciously.

In the past, when I've expressed this message, some people have reacted angrily and said that this somehow denies the existence of God as the Source. Please understand that this is not a religious book, and I am in no way denying the existence of God. In fact, many devout people who have believed all their lives that God works and expresses through them now realize that by blaming the will of God for their problems, they are just finding another excuse. They're just inventing another way to be on the *effect* rather than the *cause* side of their lives.

When these people learn The Ultimate Secret, they see that if you believe God is the Source, and the

Source is on your side, working through you, you don't ever have an excuse to plead helplessness again.

Whether you believe in God or not, as long as you look at a situation and say, "I didn't create *this*," you're allowing the situation to remain beyond your control. You're saying there's nothing you can do about it, that it must remain so forever—or until somebody else changes it for you.

But as soon as you say, "I did create this," you make it your own. You accept sole responsibility. When you accept responsibility for *creating* a situation, you're then ready to assume responsibility for *changing* it. And when you assume responsibility for changing it, you take control of your life.

This approach works no matter how old you are, what kind of physical shape you're in, how much money or education you have, where you live, whom you know, or what you've done in the past. All that matters is what goes on in your head.

Once again, the steps are:

- Accept responsibility for having created things the way they are,
- Assume responsibility for changing them,
- Take control.

If you'll recall, I said that The Ultimate Secret does not demand that you actually *do* anything. Note that none of the above steps require any physical action on your part. They do not constitute a how-to formula. They are merely shifts in your attitude or your mental set. Together they constitute the vital, crucial beginning of an entirely new approach to life—an approach in which *you* are the cause of what happens.

CHAPTER SIX

What You Need

To move from your start, which we have defined as the taking of control, to your destination, which is the achievement of a desire or goal, you need only two things:

1. A clear idea of what you want (an objective). For some people, this is easy. From the time they were children, such people have had a detailed mental picture of their desired objective, their life's goal. For these fortunate ones, the process of forming a clear idea of what they want is merely a matter of calling up a mental picture and concentrating on it. For most of the rest of us, however, it's not that simple.

An idea, in this process, is nothing more than a mental picture, which you send to your subconscious mind. But be advised: The subconscious mind does not respond well to fuzzy pictures. The subconscious mind responds best to sharp, clear, specific ideas. Just saying to yourself, "I want a lot of money," probably isn't clear enough. It's better to say exactly how much money. Nor is it enough to say, "I want a new job." The world is full of jobs. Say exactly what kind of job you want, with what kind of duties, in what kind of organization. It's helpful to write down what you want in words that are as specific as you can make them. If you, like many people, are not quite sure what you want, state very clearly your *intention to discover* exactly what you desire in a specific area of your life, by a certain point in time.

Remember, the subconscious mind does not care

what kind of idea you present to it, as long as that idea is sharp, clear, and specific.

2. Commitment. This, like willingness, is an attitude. The trouble is, it's one of the most misunderstood attitudes you've ever had to deal with. When the word "commitment" is mentioned, most people think of it as a promise or obligation. They see the promise as being imposed by someone else, as in, "I want your commitment to do this." Or they see it as a self-imposed obligation, as in, "You have my commitment to you on this."

If that's what comes to mind for you when you hear the word "commitment," I'm going to ask you to change the way you think of it. Most people I know who have used this new definition report that it works much better in their lives.

Commitment, according to this new definition, is a *feeling of confidence* that you'll continue to pursue what you want, no matter what happens. It's not a promise or an obligation. Rather, it's a firm belief that what you want is so desirable and so important to you that, in the end, it will be worth doing whatever you must do to get it.

This confidence—this firm, unwavering belief—is what The Ultimate Secret is all about.

CHAPTER SEVEN

What You Don't Need

While the list of things you *do* need has only two items on it (a clear objective and commitment), the list of things you *don't need* is almost endless. You *don't need* a lot of money, or time, or luck. You *don't need* a great deal of intelligence or education. The amount of intelligence it took you to read this book so far is more than enough to enable you to get absolutely everything you want for the rest of your life.

While it would be good to get help from other people, you *don't need* it. And while it would be good to have a plan of action, you *don't need* that either.

When I tell people this, they usually say, "Wait a minute. This runs contrary to everything we've heard about the rules of success. 'Plan your work, and work your plan' is the accepted wisdom."

Well, I disagree. In my years as a financial writer, I've interviewed some of the most successful people in the fields of investment, insurance, and banking. Some of these people told me they owed their success to a grand plan carefully followed. Yet many others, just as successful, say they don't like to plan and despise making lists of things to do. They simply have a goal, and follow their instincts in working toward it.

There's a reason you don't need plans; a powerful reason, rooted in a powerful principle. The reason is that when you have a clear objective and a commitment to reaching it, you'll *naturally* be drawn to doing the things that move you toward that objective.

In other words, you have a natural, automatic, built-in mechanism that tells you what to do in order to get what you want. The mechanism works even though you haven't the vaguest idea how to get the objective. All you have to do is fix the objective clearly in your mind and commit to achieving it. The *process*—the how-to—will take care of itself! The process will come out of your intention to achieve the objective. You'll know, naturally, what to do, how, and when. And what you don't know naturally, you'll learn—with ease.

Earlier I said some things about how-to books that might suggest to you that I think they're of little value. Not at all. The written word has great value to people who (1) know what they want, and (2) are committed to getting it. For such people, how-to books and articles are marvelous shortcuts on the roads to their objectives. In fact, once you have the objective and the commitment, the built-in mechanism I just mentioned will often attract you to the exact how-to book or article that will help you the most.

What I'm trying to get you away from is an undue emphasis or reliance on how-to processes. Look at the processes people use to get anything. No matter how cut-and-dried these processes seem, all are at least somewhat arbitrary.

Consider the process of getting a bachelor's degree. At first, it would seem that to get a degree you must go through the process of attending classes for four years, taking tests, and getting passing grades in all those classes.

Now, look at how many people have gotten bachelor's degrees by mail-order. Look at the number who have attended classes and gotten credit but didn't take a test. Besides that number, how many have skipped the classes and just taken the tests? How many have gotten credits for their work or life experience, thereby skipping the class-and-test process altogether? I myself used several of these devices to complete a bachelor's degree from a Big Ten university in less than four years, and without actually attending many of the classes that I successfully passed.

Thus, we see that the process is to a certain extent arbitrary. In the case of a college degree, it may be totally happenstance. Look at *any* process—right now—and note how much of it is arbitrary. How many of the steps in the process were invented by someone for reasons long since obsolete or forgotten—and are thus partly or entirely optional?

What organization is more attached to its "processes" than the United States government? And which agency of that government is more in love with its processes than the Internal Revenue Service? Well, let me tell you a story that may lead you to doubt forever the necessity of processes.

I once worked for an organization that gave aid to disadvantaged youth. One day, my boss rushed into my office, delighted by the news that none other than Mr. Henry Ford II wanted to make a very large contribution to our organization. But, Mr. Ford wanted the contribution to be tax-deductible. The problem was, our organization was not qualified with the Internal Revenue Service; in other words contributions made to us were *not* tax-deductible.

Because I was a law student at the time, my boss assigned me the task of securing tax-deductible status for our organization by the end of Mr. Ford's taxable year, which was only a few days away. I called the IRS and was told by a clerk that getting approval as a tax-deductible charity routinely took six months—and that the normal process could not be waived. I was crestfallen. I told my boss that the approval was impossible to get in a few days.

What I didn't know was that my boss was a master of The Ultimate Secret. He had a clear *objective:* he wanted that contribution. And he had the *commitment:* he was willing to do whatever it would take to get that contribution. His reply to me was, "I don't care what some clerk says. I want tax-exempt status for this organization, and I want it *tomorrow*! Let's do what we have to, but let's get that approval."

I tried to reason with him, but to my amazement and frustration, he seemed to have gone selectively deaf. All he could hear was, "OK, I'll try again."

I got back on the phone and explained the situation to the same clerk. First, he just laughed. Then he patiently explained to me why my request was impossible. But after talking with my boss, I too had gone selectively deaf. I just wouldn't hear the word "impossible," no matter how many times he said it. When he finally realized I wasn't going to give up, he referred me to another clerk, who referred me to yet another clerk, who at long last referred me to an application examiner. After I had told my story for what seemed to be the tenth time, and for the tenth time refused to accept no for an answer, the examiner agreed to talk to his supervisor and then get back to me. I hung up and crossed my fingers. The time was about 10:00 A.M.

A half hour later, the examiner called and said in a strained and uncomfortable voice, "This is highly, highly irregular. We hate to do things this way. I hesitate to even tell you about it over the phone. We can't afford to let word of this get out. But . . ."

"But what?" I asked, nearly bursting.

He replied in a rush, as if he hoped I wouldn't understand. "If you can have the application form filled out and delivered by 5:00 P.M. today, I'll review it, and if everything's in order, I can give you preliminary approval by 5:00 tomorrow. We'll waive the full investigation for now and issue a final ruling in due course. However, once the preliminary approval has been signed, contributions to your organization will be tax-deductible immediately."

"Meaning we can accept the contribution tomorrow?"

His reluctance made his voice heavy. "Yes."

When I told my boss, he literally jumped out of his chair. We rushed to the IRS office and got the form. To my utter horror, it was ten pages long and asked questions that I had no idea how to answer. But knowing my boss, I didn't even try to make excuses.

As I sat mulling over the endless questions on the form, my wife called, and I told her my predicament. Her voice brightened. "Hey, a friend of mine, a woman who helped put together our women's professional organization, had to fill out that same form a couple of years ago. I'll bet she could help. And she works in the very same building you're in. Maybe if you call her right now . . ."

Before she could finish, I thanked her, we hung up, and I called her friend. Sure enough, she had filled out the form, and yes, she would be happy to help. Minutes later, she came up to my office, and together we got it done.

When the last photocopy was made, and we looked at the clock, our elation quickly turned to despair when we realized that we had just five minutes to get the form to the IRS. The Federal Building was at least ten minutes away, through downtown rush-hour traffic.

Panic-stricken, I rushed into my boss's office and found him chatting with a police officer in uniform. Quickly, I explained the problem. My boss looked at the police officer and asked, "Could you take him over in your patrol car, with the light and siren going?"

"Only if it's an emergency," the officer replied.

My boss stood up. "Look, if we don't get this form to the IRS in"—he checked his watch—"four minutes, a lot of unfortunate kids are going to lose out on the biggest pile of money this organization's ever seen."

"Sounds like an emergency to me," the officer agreed, smiling devilishly. We were off.

For the next few minutes, my heart pounded in my throat as we wove our way through five-o'clock traffic, with the scream of the siren bounding off the buildings all around us and the patrol car's blue light sweeping our path clean. We never went more than twenty-five miles an hour, yet thanks to the siren and light, we never had to stop, and arrived at the Federal Building with one minute to spare.

At 4:45 P.M. the next day, my boss and I were sitting in the office of the District Director of the IRS, who signed the preliminary approval of our status. Mr. Ford wrote his check and got his deduction. We got the largest single contribution in the history of our organization. All this, without experience, without a plan, and in the face of an "unwaivable" six-month government process.

So much for plans and processes. They might be nice to have, but you don't need them. *Objective* and *commitment* are everything.

CHAPTER EIGHT

How the Principle Works

Once again, The Ultimate Secret is this: In order to accomplish something, you must be willing to do whatever it takes to accomplish it. In a nutshell, that's the whole thing—and it works. It works for me, for you, for everyone who uses it, millions of times every day.

It works naturally, whether you understand it or not. To use it and benefit from it, you don't have to understand it, any more than you have to understand electricity in order to use and benefit from an electric light. When certain conditions are present, it works automatically, whether you believe in it or not. As you turn on an electric light, you may not believe that the current flows through the wires, but the light goes on anyway. So it is with The Ultimate Secret.

Even though understanding and belief are not necessary, I've found that some people—especially those who consider themselves "realistic" or skeptical—are more willing to accept and use the principle if they understand just how it works. For those people, I'd like to describe the mechanism through which The Ultimate Secret takes a simple attitude called *willingness* and uses it to produce the most complex and momentous results.

The mechanism behind this principle brings four elements into play. They are:

1. a concept,
2. a law,
3. a phenomenon, and
4. a power.

1. THE CONCEPT OF THOUGHTS AS THINGS

If you're like most people, you put thoughts into the nonphysical category. You consider your thoughts to be "mental," as opposed to physical. You can't see, touch, or measure them. There's no way you can prove to anyone that you have them. Of course, you can write your thoughts down or draw pictures of them, but the words and pictures are not the actual thoughts; they're only symbols of what you're thinking.

Yet even though you can't see, touch, or measure your thoughts, you know they exist—you know that they're real—because you *think* them. In the same way, you know that love exists—that love is real—because you feel it.

Few people will deny the reality of such seeming intangibles as thoughts, ideas, feelings, and emotions. What most people *do* deny, however, is the *physical* reality of thoughts. They believe that thoughts exist "only in the mind," on some nonphysical plane, as if the mind were nowhere. Since thoughts can't be physically observed or measured, they reason, thoughts don't physically exist.

But let me ask them—and you—this: What if thoughts *do* have a physical reality? What if they *are* physical "things"—as real as the book you're reading or the hand you're holding it with?

The answer is, if thoughts do exist on the physical plane, if they are actual "things," then they would be subject to the same laws of nature that affect all other physical things. And they would behave in the same ways.

I wish I could prove to you, scientifically, that thoughts *are* physically real. Unfortunately, I can't. As of the time I'm writing this, many scientists believe that thoughts are actually physical phenomena, but as yet they've not developed instruments capable of measuring thoughts in any concrete way.

There are instruments (such as the polygraph and biofeedback machines) that can measure the physical *effects* of your thoughts. But they cannot show the thoughts themselves, just as there are instruments that can measure the effects of electrons flowing through wire but cannot show the electrons themselves.

When you and I want to put electricity to work, we do it even though we can't see the electron. We proceed on what we know and use it in the best way we can. I ask you to join me in doing exactly the same thing with The Ultimate Secret. By the way, when we do this, we'll be in very good company.

When we use The Ultimate Secret, we join forces

with a number of enlightened thinkers who, over the ages, have operated on the assumption that thoughts are indeed physically "real." From ancient times, such people have believed that their thoughts have an objective reality, an existence apart from the mind that conceived them. In other words, to these people, thoughts are *things*.

Let's operate on that assumption too. Let's assume that when you think something, when you form a thought in your mind, it takes on a physical form and an existence of its own. Whether you form the thought carefully or casually, whether you think it intensely or lightly, whether you consciously drag it up or it springs up by accident—the moment you think it, your thought is physically *real*. It's a *thing*.

Well, so what? Why is it important that "thoughts are things"? Think back to our earlier discussion. Remember, we said that if thoughts are physical things, then they would fall within the operation of the same physical laws that govern every single thing in the entire universe. And for our purposes, one of those universal laws is extremely important. It's the law of attraction.

2. THE LAW OF ATTRACTION

Simply stated, the law is this: Things attract other things. Evidence of this abounds in nature. From the largest planets to the tiniest microbes, attraction rules them all. Attraction keeps the planets in orbit, preventing them from flying off into space. Indeed, if they weren't being held apart by other forces, the law of attraction, unchecked, would cause the planets to come zooming together.

Scientists have a name for this law. It's called gravitation, and it's defined as the "mutual attraction of any two bodies." That's *any* two bodies, *any* two physical things.

There's even a formula that expresses the force of this attraction in mathematical terms:

$$F = \frac{GM_1M_2}{R^2}$$

Even if you have no head for math, this formula is very easy to understand. *F* is the force of attraction between two things. *G* is just a number, something called a "mathematical constant," which never changes. The two *M*'s are the masses of the two things being attracted to each other, and the *R* is the distance between them. R^2 is that distance squared (multiplied by itself).

When you multiply the mass (or size) of the two things times each other and times the constant, then divide by the squared distance between them, you can actually measure the force of attraction pulling them together. This force is at work at all times, drawing all things toward one another.

Remember, things attract other things. When applied to thoughts, the law means that, by some process that we don't fully understand, *whenever you think something, the thought immediately attracts its physical equivalent.*

Think about eating, and soon you're hungry. If there's food around, before you know it, you're eating. Think about something sad, and soon you're feeling sad, maybe even crying. The thought, which you can't see or measure, attracts its physical equivalent, which you can.

Every book that's ever been written on the subject of positive attitudes has preached this gospel: To win, you must think about winning. To succeed, you must think success. What you think about, comes about. Napoleon Hill, the writer who revolutionized the thinking of millions of people with his classic motivational book, *Think and Grow Rich,* stated his central principle thus: "What the human mind can conceive and believe, the human mind can achieve."

These "positive thinking" books are not wrong. No skeptic has ever been able to refute their central truth. The law of attraction applies to everything. In objective reality, the thought of winning attracts the physical counterpart of winning, that is, the physical activity or result that is the victory itself. The thought of success attracts its physical counterpart, be it in the form of a sales commission, a promotion, or whatever "success" means to the person thinking about it. And it's here that an amazing phenomenon comes into play.

3. THE PHENOMENON OF ACCELERATING ACCELERATION

When you think of something—let's say it's a personal fortune of ten million dollars—that thought immediately begins attracting its physical equivalent. The thought, as a "thing," immediately begins drawing ten million dollars toward itself, toward you, the holder of the thought. Now, in physical reality as you perceive it, ten million dollars may seem a long, long way from where you are. The prospect of you physically having that fortune may seem quite dim.

But never fear; you have help. It comes in the form of a phenomenon called *accelerating acceleration*. Simply described, this phenomenon is:

When things begin moving toward each other, they move at an ever-increasing rate.

Not only are the things themselves moving faster, but their *rate* of movement is getting faster with each passing moment.

When you think of having ten million dollars, that money immediately begins making its way toward you. Once it's begun, it moves faster and faster, until you can't keep track of it. Many a multimillionaire has told how it took fifteen or twenty years to make the first million, several years to make the second, a few months to make the third, then very little time for other millions to come flying in.

That's because of the phenomenon of accelerating acceleration. The law of attraction is so powerful that once things pick up momentum, they fly toward each other with increasing speed. The things you want fly toward you more quickly and easily as time goes by.

To see why this phenomenon works, let's take a second look at our formula for the law of attraction, which you'll recall was

$$F = \frac{GM_1M_2}{R^2}$$

The R, you'll remember, is the distance between the two M's, the masses of the two things being attracted to each other. The little ^{2} next to the R means the distance is multiplied by itself. When the two things get closer together, the R becomes a much smaller number.

Let's take an example. Suppose the distance, R, is 10. When you multiply 10 by itself (10 X 10), you get 100. Now let's suppose the distance is half as much, or 5. You would think that, all other factors staying the same, when the distance between the two things is cut in half, the force of attraction between them (F) would be doubled.

Not so, because when you multiply 5 by itself (5 X 5), you get 25. And 25 isn't *half* of 100, it's *one fourth* of 100.

This means, with G, M_1 and M_2 staying the same, and the distance between the two M's cut in half, then the force of attraction (F) is *four times* as great, because you are *dividing* by a number that is *one fourth* as large. When this happens, the entire effect is exaggerated. The things move toward each other much faster, because the force pulling them together is much stronger.

Now, I congratulate you if you were able to follow that discussion and understand the mathematics of this phenomenon. But if you didn't understand a word of it, don't worry. All you have to do is think the thought. Simply by saying the word, you set the law of attraction into motion. The rest is taken care of, automatically, and with accelerating acceleration.

4. THE POWER OF AN OPEN MIND

The last element of our principle is a mysterious power. It's mysterious not because it can't be understood, but because most people choose not to understand it. By the time they reach adulthood, most people have their minds made up on life's major issues and would rather not be bothered with changing their minds.

Yet an open mind is like an open window. It lets the fresh air in. An open mind allows the law of attraction to work without interference. It allows the phenomenon of accelerating acceleration to run free. When you keep an open mind, you permit your thoughts to find their physical equivalents in ways a closed mind may not have consciously thought possible.

Your open mind is a window to the limitless possibilities in the universe. It is the catalyst for chemical reactions in unbounded number and variety. It is an instrument of immense, all-encompassing power.

In the final analysis, an open mind is what makes everything else work—the concept, the law, the phenomenon, even the principle itself.

CHAPTER NINE

What Keeps the Principle from Working

As I've said before, the principle contained in this book is automatic. It works by itself. But that doesn't mean it works all the time, or that it can't be stopped. If that were the case, we'd all be running around, happily loaded down with everything we want. The fact is, people stop the principle behind The Ultimate Secret far more often than they allow it to work.

Let's say you have a clear objective: to become the president of your company within the next five years. Having read this book so far, you realize that to reach your goal, all that's necessary is that you be willing to do whatever it takes to get it.

Being the methodical type, you sit down and make a list of all the things you feel are necessary for you to reach your particular goal. (Remember you don't *have to* do anything. You don't have to make lists, though they may help organize and clarify your thinking.) For the sake of example, let's say your list looks like this:

1. Work in every department of the company.
2. Earn a college degree at night.
3. Work twelve hours a day, six days a week.

And so it goes. You continue to list all the things that you see as being necessary to the achievement of your objective . . . until you come to No. 42, which looks like this:

42. Relocate to a different city.

With a sigh of sadness, you look at No. 42 and say, "No, I'm not willing to do that. I know the headquarters is in a different city, but I like *this* town. My family is here, my friends are here, my kids are in school here. I hate packing, and I hate disruption. I won't relocate."

When you think that, *Wham!* Everything stops. In a split second, you short-circuit the principle, interfere with the law of attraction, and slam the brakes on accelerating acceleration. By closing your mind to that one element, No. 42, you rob yourself of the power that makes everything else work.

When you say "I'm not willing" with respect to *any* aspect of anything it takes to get what you want, you instantly shut down the powerful mechanism that was automatically starting to bring your goal to you. When you say, "I'm not willing to do that," you close your mind. In effect, you decide that one certain, prescribed way is *the* way things must be or must not be. You perceive certain barriers as permanent. With your mind closed, nothing works.

Right now, you might be saying to yourself, "Wait a minute. Let's try. Let's start doing the items on the list. Maybe No. 42 won't ever come up and I won't have to move."

My response is this: Whatever your barrier is, whatever you're unwilling to do, that barrier will come up without fail. In fact, it will come up early—maybe even the very first thing. I don't know why it seems to work that way. Perhaps it's the built-in economy of nature. Circumstances seem to highlight the one item that's jamming up the works. It could be a sort of Murphy's Law: If something *can* go wrong, it *will*. If something *can* stop the principle, it *will*—and it will come up soon.

So, if you set a goal and find that it involves something that you're unwilling to do, you might as well save yourself a lot of time and trouble. Forget that goal and start looking at others. There are plenty of worthy goals in this world. You'll find another.

Is this a defeatist attitude? Is it negative? Is it discouraging and disheartening? Actually, no, and here's why.

There's an opposite side to this particular Murphy's Law—a side that will throw open the floodgates to your accomplishment. It's this: When you become committed, when you become absolutely clear in your own mind that you are willing to do whatever it takes to achieve your goal, the mechanism—the *principle*—starts creating shortcuts for you. It starts eliminating the need to do certain items. It brings your goal to you with accelerating acceleration and without nearly all the trouble you thought was necessary.

Those are my words. For a much more poetic description of the same phenomenon, savor the words of the German literary giant, Johann Wolfgang von Goethe:

Until one is committed, there is hesitancy, the chance to draw back, always ineffectiveness. Concerning all acts of initiative (and creation) there is one elementary truth the ignorance of which kills countless ideas and splendid plans: that moment one definitely commits oneself, then Providence moves too.

All sorts of things occur to help one that would never otherwise have occurred. A whole stream of events issues from the decision, raising in one's favor all manner of unforeseen incidents and meetings and material assistance, which no man could have dreamed would come his way.

If you want to be company president in five years, and if reaching that goal involves forty-two items, you must be willing to do all forty-two of them. But once you commit to doing all forty-two of them, the chances of your actually having to do them all dramatically decrease. You may not have to get a college degree. You may not have to work twelve hours a day.

You may *never* have to relocate. The trouble is, when you set your goal, you don't know in advance which items on the list will be eliminated. *That's* why you must be willing to do every one!

As I was writing this book, a friend of mine told me the story of how the principle worked for her. About five years ago, she was living in an apartment she didn't care for, and so she began the arduous task of apartment hunting in a city where nice apartments were pitifully scarce. After much searching, she found a beautiful apartment complex that had everything she wanted—including a nine-hole golf course, and my friend loves to play golf. When she inquired about moving in, the manager told her that apartments did come open now and then and were filled by the management calling people whose names were on a waiting list. She could fill out an application and add her name to that list, but should expect a wait of probably two years.

"Isn't there any way I can move in sooner?" my friend asked.

"Possibly," the manager replied. "Sometimes I'll get a vacancy, but the next people up on the list can't move in right away. If someone farther down the list can move immediately, I'll put them in first."

"Great. How can I know when that happens?"

"The only way to find out is to stop in here every day," he said. "I'm so busy I just can't accept telephone inquiries about vacancies."

The prospect of making the same inquiry, day after day, with no guarantee of success discouraged my friend. "Well, I'm certainly not willing to drive over here every day," she said, and she began looking elsewhere.

In the next five years, she lived in five different apartments and was unhappy with each. When she learned that her rent was about to be raised again, she decided to go back to the building she had loved so much five years before. But this time she resolved that she would do whatever was necessary to get in.

In a conversation with the manager, she learned that the building was still full, that there was a two-inch stack of applications ahead of hers, and that the only way to get in sooner was by dropping into the office every day and inquiring in person, just as she was told five years before.

"You might have to come in here every day for months and months," the manager explained. "And even then, I can't guarantee you'll get an apartment."

"That's all right," my friend said. "I'm willing to do whatever it takes."

That was Friday. On Saturday and Sunday, the office was closed. On Monday, at one minute after nine in the morning, my friend's phone rang. "I have an apartment open," the manager said with a big smile in his voice. "And I got to thinking how, in a way, you've been on this waiting list for five years already, and since you wanted an apartment so bad, you were ready to come up here every day, and, well, if you can move in right away . . ."

With her heart racing, my friend answered, "If that's what it takes, I'll do it!"

There's nothing strange about this story—others like it take place countless times every day. My friend was merely using the principle to her advantage. She was willing to do everything it took to get what she wanted. The principle then went to work and made the job so easy she actually had to *do* very little. By the way, this took place quite a few years ago, and she still lives in that apartment, happy as can be.

Of course, things could have been different. She could have gone to that office every day, wasting her time and gasoline, and an apartment may not have opened up for months, maybe even years. She could have had her patience tested to its limit and her commitment challenged every time she heard, "Sorry, nothing today." Those kinds of stories are common, too.

Unfortunately, when you make up your mind that you want something, you never know how much will be required of you. So I can't guarantee that it will be easy. But I can guarantee that if you know and use The Ultimate Secret—if you commit to doing whatever it takes—your journey will be much easier than it would have been if you had stayed uncommitted.

By now, you know the Secret fairly well. The way you use it is simply by being willing to do every item on the list of what it takes—and then not even worry about the list. If you're not sure how much is involved in getting to your goal, just commit yourself to it. You'll find out what it takes soon enough.

It's not the knowing of every possible item, it's your *willingness* to do them that gets the principle going.

The mechanism then starts bringing your goal to you with ease, shortcuts and accelerating acceleration.

It is your willingness that will open your mind to unlimited possibilities. Without that willingness on your part, the mechanism stops. You can toil for years on the other items, but as long as you remain unwilling to do just one item, the goal will always seem farther and farther away. *Willingness* is the key. If you have it, you can get anything. If you don't, you won't.

It's that simple.

CHAPTER TEN

The Tyranny of the Accomplished Goal

This, then, is The Ultimate Secret to Getting Absolutely Everything You Want: *Know what you want and be willing to do whatever it takes to get it.* You probably won't have to do all the things. In fact, you'll probably only have to do just a fraction of them. But be willing nevertheless.

Now you have the Secret. Now you can go out and get whatever you want. With the Secret to guide and inspire you, it's inevitable: sooner or later, you *will* get what you want. Only the time it will take and the actual processes you will use are uncertain. But a word of caution. Accomplished goals can be wonderful, but they have a certain "tyranny" in them. If you begin to view your accomplishments as the prize in life, you can get hooked on them—like an addict, wanting more, only to be disappointed once you get them.

Why is that? For the simple reason that the attainment of a goal is almost never as good as you imagined it would be. Even if it is as good—even if it's better—the attainment is a momentary thing. The duration is painfully short. In no time at all, you'll begin looking for another goal to shoot for, another accomplishment to put into your trophy case. You become the victim of a tyranny—and that tyranny is your own accomplished goal.

Sad to say, we have many examples of this tyranny in modern life. Many athletes, movie stars, musicians and entrepreneurs have, through incredible talent and commitment, made it to the top of their fields in a very short time. They achieve fame, fortune, and success before most of their peers have even finished school.

And yet we read about them in the papers. Rock music stars die of heroin overdoses. A bright new comedian commits suicide. Dozens of major league baseball players are indicted for dealing in cocaine. These are people who reached the top, looked around, and couldn't see anything else. It's not something you want to have happen in your life.

Someone once asked a famous scientist, "What do you do once you've won the Nobel Prize?"

The scientist, who indeed had won that prize some years before, quickly replied, "Switch fields."

In other words, once you've accomplished a goal in one area of your life, go to work in another area. Many successful athletes have gone on to become just as successful in coaching, sportscasting, acting, or business. Many successful business people have retired early and used their free time to develop into prominent artists or musicians. For many years, the concert band of a large American city was conducted by a man who had been a successful attorney, then quit at the pinnacle of his career to pursue his love of music.

I've gone out of my way to make this point because I know that once you begin using the Secret you will begin accomplishing goals faster and more easily than ever before in your life. When that happens, you need to be ready for success and should have some idea of how to deal with it. Keep this in the back of your mind; you may have to put it to use sooner than you think.

CHAPTER ELEVEN

The Endless Joy
of the Journey

Once you've learned to use this Secret, you'll soon find that your greatest reward is not in the actual attainment of your goals but in the journey you undertake in going after them. I'm sure you've heard this before, but it's true: Life is not a destination; it's a journey. It's not a series of goals; it's a series of steps, of events unfolding as you make your way. Life is not all about accomplishment; it's all about doing, participating, progressing, growing, learning.

The perfect analogy for this lesson is mountain-climbing. I have some friends whose favorite pastime involves scrambling up the sides of huge boulders, scraping the skin off every knuckle, dangling from ropes thousands of feet from the ground, risking serious injury or death at every step. And for what?

"Is sitting at the top of a mountain such a thrill that it's worth all the effort and the danger?" I once asked some climbers.

"Of course not," one of them replied. "Sitting at the top is only a momentary thing. It feels good for a few seconds. You whoop and holler a little, and take in the view. But soon you get cold, and you start thinking about how long it'll take to get down."

"Then what's the big attraction of mountain-climbing?" I wondered.

"It's *climbing* to the top," he said. "Not being at the top. If you don't enjoy the climb, if you don't live for the climb, forget it. Being at the top just isn't worth all the trouble."

If you want to win a gold medal in the Olympics, you must start training in an event that you love. If you want to win as a runner, you must love the act of running. Because running is what you'll be doing—in good weather and bad, day after day, month after month, for years. Your victory, if you attain it, will last only for a few moments, just as the exhilaration of reaching the top of a mountain disappears almost instantly. After that, if you want another victory, you'll have to start training again. So you'd better enjoy it.

While goals disappear the moment you achieve them, the journey never disappears. It goes on forever—as does the joy that you experience along the way. If you approach life with that attitude, it becomes not a string of achievements, and not a rule of tyranny. It becomes a continuous, joyous adventure. And if we can make our lives be that, what more could we possibly want?

CHAPTER TWELVE

Begin It Now

For years, I've been giving speeches about The Ultimate Secret, and when I do, I usually end my talk right here. But I've noticed that, more often than not, the audience is waiting to hear something else, just a bit more to send them on their way.

"What else can I say?" I've asked myself again and again. "I've given them the Secret, shown them how to use it, cautioned them about goals, and reminded them about the joy of the journey. What else is there?"

Then a friend of mine, a professional speaker in fact, sent me a copy of the Goethe quote that you read earlier. When I read it, I was thrilled that it explained the Secret so brilliantly. But tacked onto that explanation was a bit of advice that I had not been giving—advice that you can, of course, ignore or heed, as you wish. I can predict what will happen in either case. If you ignore it, you'll soon forget The Ultimate Secret and your life will go along pretty much as it has up to now. On the other hand, if you heed the advice, your life will never be the same again. Here's what Goethe said: Whatever you can do or dream you can, begin it. Boldness has genius, power and magic in it.

Begin it now.

ABOUT THE AUTHOR

Mike Hernacki began careers in teaching, advertising, law, and stock brokerage before giving in to a long-suppressed desire and becoming a freelance writer in 1979. Since then, he ran a successful writing company, was a professional speaker, and, by living the principles described in his books, was able to "retire" in his mid-fifties. Today, he is a personal success coach and consultant to high-achieving individuals, does volunteer work for San Diego charities, and plays a lot of tennis. He and his wife, Wanda, have been happily married since 1966.

Photo by Victor Avila

ABOUT THE AUTHOR

Mike Hernacki began careers in teaching, advertising, law, and stock brokerage before giving in to a long-suppressed desire and becoming a freelance writer. Since then, he has run a successful writing company, was a professional speaker, and, by living the principles described in his books, was able to "retire" in his mid-fifties. He has written several books, some of which have been published in more than one language, including *The Secret to Permanent Prosperity, The Forgotten Secret to Phenomenal Success,* and *The Secret to Conquering Fear,* all available from Pelican.

Today, Hernacki is a personal success coach and consultant to high-achieving individuals, does volunteer work for San Diego charities, and plays a lot of tennis. He and his wife, Wanda, have been happily married since 1966.

CPSIA information can be obtained
at www.ICGtesting.com
Printed in the USA
FFOW05n0423231214